FIND THE ANIMAL

GOD MADE SOMETHING TALL

There is a merekat hiding in this book. See if you can find her.

PENNY REEVE
ILLUSTRATED BY ROGER DE KLERK

CF4•K

For Lacey

Are you ready for another adventure? Let's see what we can find. It's something God has made. It's something tall.

Praise the Lord from the heavens, praise him in the heights above.
Psalm 148:1

What are these? They are legs. God gave this tall animal four long, spotted legs. It can walk, it can run, but it can't lie down for very long.

Where is the desert rat?

If I go up to the heavens, you are there. Psalm 139:8

Can you see a square?

What do you think this is? It's a tail. God gave this tall animal a long tail for shooing away bothersome bugs.

Where is the triangle?

How great is the love the Father has lavished on us. 1 John 3:1

Can the rat reach the giraffe's tail?

What might that be? It's a neck, and even more neck! God gave this tall animal a very long neck that can reach the tops of the tallest trees.

What is the elephant doing?

Neither height nor depth ... will be able to separate us from the love of God.
Romans 8:39

Can you see a circle?

What's that? It's a tongue. God gave this tall animal a long flexible tongue to find the tastiest leaves, wherever they are, and snap them off for lunch.

What shape is on the girl's shirt?

This is how God showed his love among us; He sent his one and only son.
1 John 4:9

Can the girl reach the tallest branch?

Do you know which animal we've found? Yes, it's a giraffe. And who made it? Our great God!

Can you see a star?

We have peace with God through our Lord Jesus Christ.
Romans 5:1

Who can reach the red flower?

The giraffe is a very tall animal. It has a long neck that can reach almost all the leaves on the highest branches. Did you know God's love can reach much further than that? God's love can reach us all the time - no matter where we are, or what we've done.

Who has the banana?

He who began a good work in you will carry it on to completion until the day of Jesus Christ. Philippians 1:6

What shapes are on the picnic mat?

Thank you God for Jesus, and what he did on the cross to make me your friend. Thank you that your great love can reach and save even me.

"I pray that you, being rooted and established in love, may have power ... to grasp how wide and long and high and deep is the love of Christ." Ephesians 3:17-18